Success Over Everything

"Success Comes First"

by

Joshua Armah

A.K.A.

J Armah The Boss

This Book is Dedicated to

My Beloved Mother Diane

&

My Son Jolonnie

Armah Publishing Group

"CREATING THE BLUEPRINT FOR SUCCESS"

Books may be purchased by contacting the
publisher and author at:

www.armahpublishing.com

www.joshuaarmah.com

Publisher:

Armah Publishing Group LLC

ISBN:

978-0-9863450-0-5

First Edition

Printed in United States

Library of Congress Control Number
2015909362

Table Of Contents

Acknowledgments

Foremost I'd like to thank God for the opportunity to craft this masterpiece. Without God's Blessing this would not have been possible. Next my mother was a big inspiration for me growing up, and this book is dedicated to all her hard work, and lessons which she taught me as a child. My son truly inspired me to write this because many children of the next generation don't have few positive outlets in today's society. Big shout out to all my family, and childhood friends who I still am connected to. To all my business associates who believed in me during this process. This book truly is for the people, and the world at large. I pray that God allows us all to prosper in whatever endeavors we partake on. I am very sincere in saying I want the best for everyone. Whether you be young, old, or a newborn baby this book was made to give a blueprint and mantra of how to become successful. This is a commitment for every person who desires to be successful and wants to reap the benefits of success. To achieve this process must be accomplished.

Introduction

The journey we call life is a never ending battle of wins and losses. The time to get to the level of success we desire can take an entire lifetime for some. Many entrepreneurs spend their days and nights pondering on ways to accomplish their goals. The endless struggles we face to reach these goals are incomparable to the past. We must interpret the future through our own eyes while assuming we know what it takes to become successful.

A truly organized person can find within their self the balanced approach necessary to be progressive. Success is a process of trial and error. Similar to long winded breath that many of us take daily. As if we are track runners competing against each other in a relay race. We are all racing to the finish line.

This finish line is an objective we all have. Being first in the race of life consumes many minds daily as if it is the only important aspect of our existence. We may even overlook the small things in life for the achievement of the bigger picture. Our flaws can't be measured by the opinions of men. We must analyze our situation individually by the results of our own actions. The best way to get to the top is to find the fighting spirit within your body. Use your spirit as much as you can to get ahead in life.

The smartest people aren't necessarily the ones who succeed the most. Having the heart of a lion gets you above and beyond in the game called life. The ones you love may abandon you in this journey, and your circle may become small. In the process to succeed you have to stay strong and never surrender.

Success Over Everything or S.O.E. is a mantra to live by to give your dreams life. To manifest your destiny, God has given you a blueprint to follow. We follow the steps of the ones who have succeeded before you while paying attention to God's signs is the route that should be taken. This will get you the ultimate inspiration you need to fuel your ambition to be written in the history books.

Compare your life to a map, and your mind is the compass. Navigate through the jungle of life to get to the destination you are searching for. Too many people give up before they finish the race. You may be 95% done, and then suddenly you give up your rights to the championship by quitting.

Many people have given up in the race of life, and few have finished the race to go on to the next round. Treat this how you know it should be treated. In this manual I will give the perspective of my life, and the facts backed up by my method. I ask you to open your eyes to a new way of life, a new thought process.

To gain the jewels of this manual you must empty your cup. Be open to the possibilities that can be brought through following the instructions of this manual. Everyone has a purpose in life, and to fulfill your purpose you must stay open to grow.

Growing and evolving is an essential tool in growing the building blocks to your life. Every action we take is similar to planting a seed.

Chapter 1
Successful Mindset

I grew up with a lot of challenges in my life. I had to face a lot of adversities to become successful. As a teenager I was very rebellious, this started at the age of 14. I ran away from home to lead a life in the streets. I was continuously trying to impress others by showing off how tough I was and how much money I could get. I did whatever it took to be accepted by my peers.

This mindset was something I didn't recognize at the time due to being so focused on trying to please others. My loyalty was the sole purpose of my existence. The crew I ran with was from the same neighborhood I grew up in, and it became a habit for me to come outside on a daily basis to commit mischief.

In this phase of my life I knew that I needed to be strong to survive in the cold streets. I had homeless nights and had nights where I had to rent hotel rooms to have a place to sleep. My life was a tornado. Every day was like being stuck in a hurricane with no shelter or umbrella with limited resources.

This turned me into a soldier. It gave me the mentality to become resourceful with what I had versus trying to find additional outlets to help me.

This mindset is what I labeled the **"infinite tool"**. I labeled this the infinite tool because when you are using your brain to survive it allows you to explore into the wonderful mystery of thoughts and processes. Statistics show that the average human only uses 5%-10% of the capacity of their brain. This automatically places a deficiency on our daily capabilities because it shows we don't tap into our full potential.

I had to learn how to turn nothing into something. This is using a creative part of the brain to achieve results without having access to everything needed to complete each goal. As a teenager I had to learn the hard way how to correlate my existence in the world with my passion to be somebody.

I had an unfortunate tragedy happen during my 14th year on this earth. I was struck with a baseball bat that permanently scarred my brain tissue and I barely made it out of this situation alive. I was struck with a bat because I wanted to prove my loyalty to a friend engaging in a fight. While this friend was being struck with an aluminum bat I jumped in the way to swing a punch, but was caught right above my eyebrow.

This experience taught me one valuable thing in life which is cause and effect. Cause and effect is a precious component of life. For example, due to my loyalty I created a cause which enables actions that led to lifelong effects of being permanently scarred negatively. Now if for instance you have a cause then there is a WHY behind your actions. A reason you're doing what you're doing.

This cause will have either positive effects or negative effects. If your cause is to graduate high school or college then you will create actions that turn into habits which will be a reason you graduate. The effects of your actions will be positive such as: recommendations from teachers to undergraduate school or graduate school, employment offers from major companies, or even setting an example for your future children of why education is important. Let's look at a negative cause such as committing illegal activities in the street such as selling narcotics. Selling narcotics can get you killed. If you live then you may get thrown in jail and catch a felony. Once a felony is on your record it is something you can't erase. This will make it hard to get a good job, get into college, vote, live in certain neighborhoods, get federal student loans or grant, etc.

The cause is the reason you're doing something. You may being doing something because you have limited options and need an outlet to survive. You may have been exposed to peer pressure. You may even have a family to take care of. Ask yourself if your reasons justify risking everything when you have other alternatives outside the current choices you are making.

You don't need to be a criminal to make bad choices. You can be a regular person and still make simple mistakes. For example, you may go party at night which causes you to wake up late for work. You get a call you are fired from your job because you are tardy. The reason you were fired is that you played hard on a work night instead of getting the proper amount of rest for the next day so you can get up early. There is both a cause and an effect in this scenario. Causes and effects are directly tied to mentality.

Your mindset navigates you to certain decisions. A child's mindset differs greatly from an adult mindset. You can be the age of 35 but still have the mindset of a child. Some people grow slow mentally. This affects their life in a negative way. As you grow and become older so will your responsibilities. To provide the right amount of growth for yourself you have to find your inner "infinite tool".

Life is full of mystery and we must dig deep within ourselves to find our full potential. So many people overlook the simple things in life which can lead to the big picture they are looking for. Over 80% of success comes from the right mindset. Thoughts are things. Your ideas will attract either positive situations or negative situations. Your mindset will lead you to success or be the reason for you failure. Schools don't teach financial intelligence or wealthy habits. To have a wealthy mind your life experiences will be your best teacher while the mistakes of others will be the signs of what not to do.

To grow mentally you have to throw your ego aside and allow your mind to stay open. A full cup spills over instantly. If you have a know it all mentality how can you allow new ideas to flourish in your mind. Sometimes our biggest disease is that we don't know that we don't even know. The same way you didn't know that you didn't know about riding a bike until you learned what a bike is then learned how to ride it.

Everything in this life has stepping stones. Each step has a specific time frame different for each person. Some people can accomplish steps quick while others may take longer to get past each individual step. A wealthy mindset allows a person to go above and beyond the normal status quo. A big difference maker for successful people is knowing their WHY. Your why is the reason behind your ambition. The reason you go out there every day to work hard to accomplish your goals. This again ties directly into cause and effect.

Your mindset is defined by your spirit. The biggest confusion is that humans may think that their mind is them but your mind is not you. We are spiritual beings. Our being is way more than the mind can comprehend. Our being is an energy that is immortal. But yet our mind is a tool we are blessed with to use. Our mind is like the GPS on our Cell phone. It is what we use to find our way to our destination in life.

Everyday's a new adventure of our journey through life. Each action we take is like an airplane. We are the pilots of our actions. We may plan to do an action but the action has to be driven through its course until complete. You never know what unexpected turns can happen in life. This shows the importance of having a wealthy mind. Your mindset will give you what you need to get to the next level. It will give you the strength you need to get through any obstacle that may occur.

The biggest fear for many go getters is the reality of failure. Nobody wants to fail or be a failure. To succeed you must go through this mental fear that haunts your mind subconsciously. Trial and error is part of path to success.

<u>Principles of Successful Mindset</u>

1. **CEO of your Life** - You're the CEO of your life. You are the boss of your destiny. You have the mental power to be a legend or to be a fool. You must choose your own outcome. To be a successful CEO you must reevaluate your life periodically to make sure you're on track to success.

2. **The Sponge Mind** - The sponge mind soaks up information like a sponge soaks up water. Example; A child's mind soaks up information quick and puts it to use. You must make learning your best friend. Create space in your

mind periodically by squeezing you sponge mind so you can soak up new information.

3. **The Shield** - Your mindset must have a mental force field in your quest for greatness. Half the battle comes from what you choose not to do. Life is a game of Chess. You must be the King on the chessboard. The King commands the board without ever having to move. It doesn't have to make the moves because it has an army of tools and resources to use. You can win a game without even lifting a finger if you use your mental shield.

4. **Imaginative Resources** - One of the biggest assets of the successful mindset is the imagination. As people grow older their imagination becomes rotten like bananas that turn brown. You must keep your imagination. The resources that your imagination can create will allow you to tap into your full potential. Your imagination is like an endless fountain of youth that you can drink from daily. No matter where you're at in life you can use imagination any day to escape your doubts and fears. This will allow you to mentally journey to your

destination before you even physically go there.

5. **The Wealthy Mindset**- A wealthy mindset produces billion dollar thoughts. A wealthy mind produces healthy habits. A wealthy mind creates a wealthy life. The difference between a wealthy mind and poor mind is Life and Death. You may find many people are brain dead. No matter how much you try to help they are aren't coming back mentally. If you aren't careful you to will reach a point mentally where you can't be helped. To have a wealthy mind you must live a wealthy life as reinforcement. Learning is a big asset for the wealthy mind. It is the lifeblood which keeps a wealthy mind rich.

These principles will assist to completely have a successful mindset. Plenty of people want to be wealthy or successful but lack the mindset for it. Your mind will guide you down the right path if you're in control or lead you the wrong way if you allow it. Everyday, you must set mental objectives to grow your mindset. Your mind is a muscle, and it needs exercise. You can build your mind into your most powerful tool and resource. We all were born with intuition. Your intuition is a natural blessing which can empower your mindset to be successful. Intuition is encoded in everyone's DNA. No one can deny this truth. To act on this knowledge alone will allow your life to flourish even without formal education or growing up with a silver spoon. If you are mentally blind then it is time to wake up. It is time to accomplish your dreams.

Chapter 2
Successful Habits

I came to a place in my life where I knew I had to change my habits. In 2010, my son was born, and this was my awakening. I needed to change my life around and become a man. This wasn't necessarily a responsibility I was ready for, but it gave me the courage to face my doubts. I immediately acted on these ideas.

I enrolled in college and gained 3 sales jobs. I worked day and night. I did whatever it took to get myself ahead in life. Being a high school dropout, I had gotten my GED at the age of 16 so it was harder for me to pursue my goals of adulthood with being a minor even in college. I did what thought was right. I stopped smoking, drinking, and even hanging out with friends. My sole focus was to become successful so I can provide for my son's future.

Unfortunately, during this process in the 2nd year of my son's life, me and my wife at the time had a big fall out due to infidelity. I didn't know what to do other than to just continue working hard at becoming successful. I didn't have all the answers, but I had a purpose.

My ex wife ended up leaving me for another man, and I became homeless. I slept in the streets at 18, nowhere to go and no resources. I hit rock bottom. I ended up leaving college without any steady income. I was in a deep state of depression which I was in denial of. I kept all of my emotions hidden from the world. Every night I would cry myself to sleep due to the pain of be separated from what I thought was my family. This experience created negative habits after I fought to have positive ones.

In this process I learned one very crucial lesson, which is habits are the roots to your success or demise. You can be successful but lose it all due to bad habits. Habits can change every once and a blue moon without you even noticing it. After a couple weeks in this condition, I woke up from my depressed mental state. I decided again that I wouldn't let any person especially any woman determine my future. I called a friend, and my friend allowed me to stay under his roof temporarily.

This action allowed me to create a series of positive actions that grew into new successful habits. I had always been an aspiring entrepreneur at the time but I never pursued it fully. It wasn't until then I gave self employment my all.

This courage created entrepreneurship habits which led me to getting an opportunity to work in corporate America with a fortune 500

company at a young age and gain valuable experience that taught me how to set myself up for success. Habits are a very important aspect of life. Your ideas become actions and your actions become habits. By having a successful mindset you can create successful habits. Every person has destructive habits, and it is important to know yourself and your habits. If you truly want to be successful, the habits you have will be a common denominator to either your success or demise.

You can't allow yourself to become a weak minded individual that has destructive habits. You are you worst enemy. If you do not fight against your negative habits you will see them destroy your life. The life of successful people can be studied. If you study the habits of wealthy people you will learn what you need to do to become wealthy yourself. Your habits are also influenced by your peers. You circle of associates will either affect your habits positively or negatives. There is a saying that if you hang with 4 broke people then you will become the 5th broke person. Yet if you hang with 4 rich people then you will become the 5th rich person.

This is a habitual effect from committing certain actions with certain people. Be at one with your inner monarch. Your spirit is destined for greatness, and if you treat yourself as royalty you will become royal. It can take 21 days to make or break a habit. With this common knowledge you should now understand that nothing is overnight. You have to consistently do the right action to eliminate the wrong actions.

Habits can be an ally if you align yourself with the right support system. No one can determine your future but you unless you give someone else the power. The biggest goal for most people is to win in life. How do you become a winner? Your habits will determine whether you are a winner or not. We are habitual creatures by nature. We were created to do consistent actions without even having to think about it. For example; when we get up and walk. Do you really need to put a lot of thought into taking each step? Do you need to slowly contemplate your arising from a chair to stand up on two feet? This is an example of our habitual nature.

We walk every day automatically because it is a pattern part of our mind's operating system. Be the leader of your destiny. You can't expect another person to take you there. There is a famous quote which is "you can take a horse to the water but you can't make it drink." This manual is the same. I can point out many of your flaws and give you a jewel to enrich your life. Without you implementing the actions it won't happen. Everyday, we are climbing up the ladder of life or we are going down. Decide if you want to win or lose. You may lose battles but the war isn't over.

You must declare war on your negative habits. You must fight consistently to defeat what is holding you back in life. This enemy is like your shadow. When you have a rich mind you can see it behind you plotting on your demise. You can plan effectively and create successful habits to conquer it. When you're poor minded it is like your shadow in the dark. You can't see it. It can attack from all angles and destroy you slowly but surely. How can you expect the moves of an invisible enemy? In life we must find our inner passion to create successful habits. The motto S.O.E. is an acronym for Success Over Everything.

S.O.E. is a way to create successful habits for your life. An affirmation which you can repeat daily to build on what you need in your life to get the confidence to complete your tasks. Our minds have habits, our heart has habits, our body has habits, and our spirit has habits. It is important to recognize how everything in our being is related. You habits aren't just actions. Your habits are a crucial part of what you need to survive in life.

For example; we must eat daily to maintain a healthy nutrition. Eating is a habit we can't deny. If we deny this habit we can die. Instead what we control is what we consume. We can eat either to have an athletic build and healthy body. Otherwise, we can eat unhealthy to become obese with an unhealthy body. You should recognize how crucial habits are to your life. You must invest in yourself and give yourself the best chance for success.

It is easy to make the wrong choice while it may be hard for you to make the right choice. It is up to you to create a mind that produces positive thoughts which produces positives actions and creates positives habits. Your thoughts will have either a positive or negative chain reaction to your habits.

Mastering your body, mind, and heart is a goal we all must have. The best part of our existence is free will. We can have the choices we want with no outside interference. You can't control everything in life, but you can control the attitude at which you approach life with. Materialistic desires don't make us happy, but the pleasures of life do. Being able to have the freedom to go shopping, to eat at a nice restaurant, and live the lifestyle we desire gives

us temporary happiness. There is no true
happiness like reaching your full potential.

Principles of Successful Habits

1. **The Power 21**- The power of 21 is a
    rule to creating a successful habit. Doing
    the same action repeatedly for 21 days
    straight will create this action into a
    habit. The whole point is to do the
    action for 21 days straight, and if you
    miss one day you must start over
    completely. For example, you want to
    exercise and make it a habit. You must
    exercise for 21 days straight to turn it
    into a habit. The power 21 will become
    an important tool for you in creating
    successful habits. It will allow you to
    gain the power you need to succeed in
    life.

2. **Positive Reinforcement** - Positive
    reinforcement is the best way to keep
    your successful habits intact after
    creating them. To have positive
    reinforcement, you must develop a
    circle of associates, or friends
    supportive of your positive changes.
    People who will push you to succeed
    and hold you accountable for your
    wrongdoings. Setting goals is the best

way to capture this. Surround yourself with objects, or environments that encourage your happiness.

3. **Schedule Habits**- Scheduling your habits will allow you to have every habit organized in your life in a balanced approach. This will allow you to keep track of your progress. Scheduling your life is a very important asset that can help you grow tremendously. You must view yourself from a third person standpoint to assess your accomplishments and downfalls. Giving yourself the best shot for success is very important. It is necessary to make your best effort in this transition. A schedule will allow your life to flow easily. If you already schedule your tasks it is important to reevaluate your schedule to make sure your life is balanced. Many people bite more than they can chew at one time. Learning how to do everything in moderation will give you a balance in everything you do.

This infinite tool will be essential in your personal development. Assessing your success by the results of your habits will give you a realistic view of where you are at on your path

to success. Staying ahead of the curve and being proactive will give you more determination to be a winner. Your will power gets you to the finish line. If you can will it then it will happen. Habits are connected to willpower. Through a series of events you will see the positive effects show up in your life. Sometimes you have to start small and build in to big actions. There is no rush. Progress is a process and getting over the hump doesn't happen overnight for everyone. Get your life in order and prioritize what comes first, second, and third.

Chapter 3
Starting The Dream

All my life I have been a dreamer. I dreamed my entire destiny out, and today I am living it. I never foreseen it happening so soon even though I'm not surprised. As a young adult I have started my business and set my own hours. Being my own boss has always been my goal. For the past three years I have achieved this goal consistently with no supplemental income. Regardless of what many said, I pushed hard for what I believe in. It definitely wasn't easy, but it was all worth it. I stopped wondering what if I do it, and just did what I set out to do.

Many people have dreams, but few see their dreams come true. Why is it that many people can't accomplish their dreams? How many get up, and actually manifest their dream? The number of people is a 1 out of 1000 ratio. It is similar to how many people want to become pro athletes with million dollar contracts but few make it. You will either get paid to build someone else's dream or you will pay yourself to build your dream. So many people overlook the importance of dream chasing that it has created speculation of the theory.

You will get nowhere in life if you don't take that first step. Initiate your dreams the same way you put the key in your ignition to start you car. To move in that vehicle you must push the pedal to the metal. Nothing happens without some sort of action behind it. Dreams are part of your story, and they are apart of your future. Dreams can give you an insight to another side of life that you have yet to see.

What do you gain in life by pursuing your dreams? Happiness, achievement, and self fulfillment are all attributes of being a dream chaser. To take the first step in your journey to the top is how you will get objectives completed. Getting to the top of the food chain in life is a goal that everyone wants to accomplish. Only the dream chasers will get there.

Having the courage to go after what isn't necessarily a reality right now is what makes life worth living. It shows our supernatural ability to use our conscious mind to create a vision and manifest it in reality. Reality is what you make it, and in order to have the life you desire you must give all your energy to accomplishing your dreams.

Dreams are part of a subconscious world that we can only see through imagination. Those who fail to open their mental eye won't get very far as a dream chaser. You must have the desire to see yourself as a winner. You must be able to envision your success right now even if you don't necessarily have it. Being able to put a mental image together will give you the ambition you need to obtain it in reality.

You have two choices when it comes to dream chasing which is taking the first step or watching someone else beat you to the punch. Life is very competitive, and we all share a world of similar ideas. You can spend an entire lifetime looking at dreams, or you can spend your life achieving them. There are so many people scared to buy into their own self belief. You are window shopping your dreams. You looking at others accomplish what you desire all the time, and your accepting this fate.

You give up before you even start. A crab has more ambition than you. You're at the lowest level on the totem pole of bottom feeders. It is a despicable trait to be a window shopper. You spend more time daydreaming than you do dream chasing. If you are pursuing your dreams then you have taken a step in the right direction.

Life has many obstacles, but in order to reach success you must manifest your dreams. It is imperative that you find the route to your destination in life. Nothing can stop you unless you let it. The biggest thinkers bring about the most action in their life. God does not give hand outs. You have to work hard to get the blessing of heaven. Every twist, turn, or thought is either one step in the right direction or in the wrong direction.

As the CEO of your life, you must make the hard decisions it takes in order to take control of your future. Many people observe from a distance, but yet they want the luxury of the wealthy. How can you accomplish anything by simply looking at it? It takes action to get to the next level in your life. The benefit of having a rich life is enormous.

When you are in tune with your destiny it will give you the ambition you need to rise above the rest. In order to find success in life go out there and get it. Everyday is a battle, and you must do your duty to get your rewards. A boss doesn't complain, they take action in times of hardship. A boss stands up to the plate, and handles their business. Don't let anything stop you from being the best that you can be. What will you assume in your journey next?

What will be your ultimate goal? How will your future play out? The biggest payout in your life will come from your own two hands. What you earn is what you deserve. Life has building blocks, and dream chasing is an endless journey. The more value that you can add to your life the bigger of an asset you will be. You must be an asset for others in order to gain the status that you seek. Perception in life controls the minds of the masses.

We are one big universe that co exists with one another in order to survive the daily struggle. Legends are born through their story, and only record breakers make the history books. Your energy to be the best at what you do will take you far places as long as you continue to build upon your future with positive goals. Connect your goals like a constellation. Some may be born stars but many lack the connection to be the constellation. Magnify your purpose in life to see everything clearly. This value will add an abundance of glory to your quest.

A strong person doesn't give up when the going gets tough. Every real boss stands up to the plate no matter the occasion. This is a universal rule in being in position of leadership. How will you assess you value without measuring the results of your actions? One plus one equals two. This is what business is all about. Everything must add up.

You circle of associates will either be assets or liabilities. No true boss can surround themselves with liabilities. The dream chaser mentality is living and breathing in millions of people. Only a select few realize its true power. Can you control your emotions, and conquer your doubts? Will your weaknesses be the reason for your demise? A true genius questions their credibility even when no one else does.

This is how you gain the momentum you need to shoot into the cosmos. The depth of the ocean can't surpass the mass of your soul. Your spirit is an immortal being with supernatural powers. You must believe in your spirit to fight through any issue. How will you reason with failure? Can you compromise your destiny for mediocrisy? It's easy to give up when you don't have a lot to lose. What will the outcome of your choices be in order to succeed?

Focus on the potential that lives within your being. Capitalize on your endeavors before they reach their peak. Find your future through seeing the present. How will you gain more than the eye can see? Draw your success on the canvas of your life. Be the artist to your vision. This is a true dream chaser. Emphasize your greatness beyond your comprehension level.

Principles of Initiating The Dream

1. **Be A Visionary-** A visionary can visualize their success even if they haven't accomplished it. The visionary has an undeniable belief in their capability to perform. The one who can see their future through imagination will

amount to greatness. Taking yourself into the realm of visionaries is no easy task. It is a daily goal which one must partake. In order to be the best you can be you have too see it first. Your mental eye will guide you through the confusion. A big thinker is a big achiever. The visionary takes everything to the next level.

2. **Create The Blueprint**- To be the architect to success you must have a blueprint. You must have your entire plan laid out on documentation. A documented plan excels in the digital era. Technology has allowed the average person to have unlimited resources. Once you tap into what you have everything will be clear. This is like a pirate following the map to a treasure chest. This is a necessary component in the mission of your destiny. Follow your nose to the smell of victory. Let no enemy prosper against your objective.

3. **Be The Pilot Of Your Plane**- Every captain must steer their ship. Every idea or plan you have is a new flight. You must be the pilot to your own aircraft. You will either get paid to build someone else's dream or pay yourself to

manifest your dream. Every adventure is a different fight. As if your boxing, each fighter is a different opponent. You have to understand what makes you unique. How can you take advantage of today's opportunities? What is your motivation for success? Every heart is full of fire. You must let this fire be the fuel to your plane. Spread your wings, and fly to your goals. Be what they say you cant. Enlighten your soul through rigorous training. There are numerous benefits throughout the plane ride, but you must notice each one of them.

A palace is built from the ground up. Your dreams are a castle waiting to be constructed. Nothing can take the place of your passion, and no one will ever be able to keep you from being a winner except yourself. To speak the dialogue necessary you must learn the language of wealthy people. A life of success happens through a consistent effort to chase your dreams.
Becoming an entrepreneur is not easy. It is a contractual agreement that you make with yourself. Financial freedom is only one small task in the overall picture. Changing the world we live in by solving the problems with viable solutions keeps our future bright. How will you

partake on your path to the top? What obstacles will you overcome? There is a lot to learn regardless of how much you know.

Chapter 4
Success Through Failure

Throughout history people have learned historical lessons through trial and error. Many of the world's greatest leaders and public figures have mentioned the attributes of their success. Trial and error has been a key for many leaders in their journey to success. Throughout my life I have failed and made mistakes. Despite my errors, I have always learned valuable lessons from the failure that I have experience.

A true visionary holds on to their dream no matter what happens. A life of poverty, hardship, and tribulations can truly test the faith of the individual going through it. Open your eyes to the reality of the world we live in by comparing and contrasting your actions with those who are successful. How do your choices measure up to the overall big picture?

The world we live in is full of losses. A strong indicator of belief stems from the desire to win. Planting your seeds is the first step to manifesting your future. Hope, love, happiness, and peace reside within the person who has let go of all materialistic desire.

In order to become a success, failure will happen more often than not. God tests us all through the struggle that we experience. In the face of adversity, you must remember all pain is temporary. Folding under pressure will do you more harm than sticking it out in tough times. You can be led to the water, but it is your choice to drink the water. You must have an appetite for success that makes you crave accomplishing your objectives day and night.

People who use their intuition will have outstanding results in their attempt to become the best that they can be. In order to complete your destiny in life you must be aware of the obstacles on your path. There are no shortcuts to success. Being diligent in your quest to greatness will bring you extraordinary rewards.

Pay attention to the warning signs that pop up spontaneously. We are what we think, and we become what we follow. My whole life changed when I became a father. The moment I found out my girlfriend at the time was pregnant, everything in my life stopped. I was only 16, and didn't know the first thing about being a father due to the fact I grew up without my father in my life. I was still in the ghetto hustling my way out. I knew that I needed to make a change fast because I didn't want to die or go to jail due to the lifestyle I was living. I immediately got my GED, enrolled in community college, and found 2 jobs to work full time.

My pregnant girlfriend at the time was depending on me for moral support throughout the pregnancy, but instead I was too busy pursuing my goal of becoming established in society. I neglected her, and it took a strain on our relationship. I thought I was making the right choices, but the constant fighting between me and my girlfriend taught me differently. I did not balance both personal and work life correctly.

When my son was finally born it gave us a new hope. We immediately shared a precious moment in the hospital, and I vowed to make a difference. At the time, I was only 17 with a lot of responsibility. I had to fill the shoes of a grown man at a young age. I decided to take the first step in securing my career in the business world. I landed a new job work as an assistant manager for a direct marketing company. This gave me even more confidence, and I added this endeavor to my already full plate.

Unfortunately, I was working close to 100 hours per week while going to college full time. This led to me rarely ever being home. The biggest mistake I made was avoiding quality time with my newly found family. I made a bigger effort by getting married to my then girlfriend, but this was an even bigger mistake. Our relationship was beyond rocky, and after only 2 months of being married it was over

. My wife at the time had found new love, and decided to choose her new found love over me. I was devastated and heart broken. I didn't understand why she cheated, but I knew I wasn't going to give up that easy. I made multiple attempts to reconcile our relationship, and almost committed suicide from the pain I felt. I failed miserably, and gave up all hope. My life went in a downward spiral. I lost all 3 of my jobs, and became homeless right after my 18th birthday. I was truly heart broken, and didn't have any outlets to turn to.

A friend who I consider family heard of the news, and immediately called me. He allowed me to temporarily move in with him until I got back on my feet. After months of grieving, I finally decided to move on.

The minute I made this decision my life bounced back. I found a new job, and manage to save up enough money to move out of my friend's apartment. This led me to having a stronger belief in myself as a man because it only made me stronger as a person.

My experience in this circumstance is an example of success through failure. Despite the infidelity of my ex wife, the hardship of poverty, and the depression of heartbreak I made it out of that situation as a bigger man.

There are many lessons to be learned in life. The application of the knowledge you have will lead you to a brighter future.

My life was a roller coaster as a teenager, and never had a moment of stability. The truth of the matter is no matter what happens in life the best teacher will be your life experience of trial and errors. The ultimate choice is yours, and if you don't take the appropriate risk to secure your legacy then everything will vanish at the blink of an eye. What you do today will determine what happens tomorrow. Survival is key in this dog eat dog world. Value yourself, and be who you say you are.

Principles of Success Through Failure

1. Strength In Numbers - The outlook you have on success should be measure by number of attempts that you took to accomplish your objective. This will allow you to analyze your patterns and habits. For example, to successfully learn to ride a bike you may attempt to ride 12 times while falling before you finally learn how to hold your balance. This will give you an estimate on how you learn and the type for learner that you are. Practice makes perfect, and in order to truly be successful you must continue to try until you successfully do what you are attempting to accomplish.

2. Name Your Price - In the world we live in everything has a price. You have to judge your decisions by what they will cost you, not just by what you will gain. Know your value, and take educated risks. No one can push you harder than yourself. Don't allow the world fill your mind with doubts, and fears. Failure has a price, and success has a price. How much is your success worth? To name your price is to set your value in the marketplace. Be priceless and the world will treat you as such. Be worthless and the world will treat you as such.

3. Sacrifice Brings Honor- Build your desire around the information of your mind. Life is full of sacrifices, obstacles, and tribulation. You must choose your path to greatness, and take action on your dream. Sacrificing time, energy, objects of desire, and more will be a test of dedication. You must abide by your vision, and use your success as a testimony. You will have to be better than your competition to succeed. Life is about the attitude you approach every scenario with. Sacrificing what you want for what you need brings you a multitude of blessings. There are very few people who make it to the level of superstardom in their chosen field. This means your sacrifice must be that much greater in order to thrive in the current playing field.

In order to manifest your vision, you must complete every objective on your list. The sacrifices you encounter may include unforeseen financial burdens, time constraints, etc. The only true loser is the one who quits. Perseverance is an attribute of true winners. The cycle of life is repetitive, and in order to get ahead of the curve you must build a momentum.

It may take years of failure to reach a notable level of success. Everyone wants to be a winner, but many are afraid to lose. The greatest legends in history have lost in many endeavors. You control your destiny! You have the power to be different! To accomplish your pursuit of happiness, you must harness all of your will power for your mission of success. Through hardship and ease, your mind is the ultimate indicator of success. If you think positive you will attract positive things. Don't give up on your future, regardless of how hard it gets on the road to greatness.

Chapter 5
Emotion, Ambition, and Motivation

In my life, my ambition has been the driving force behind a lot of my decisions. Emotion, ambition, and motivation all go hand in hand. When I first moved to New York City, I had no job outside of being an entrepreneur. This situation was the ultimate test to see how much of a hustler I really was. I decided to stick to my guns, and pursue the entertainment business full time. Everything started off shaky. I didn't have a stable income at all. While sleeping on the couch of a business associate, I would look for ways to increase my finances.

It was very hard because everything I did make from providing services as a consultant would have to be spent immediately on bills. It was so bad that I would go days without eating, or even sleeping. At the time, I had a lot of business contacts which did help me stay busy with work. Regardless of this, I did what I had to do to survive.

It got to the point where I had to pick up a gig as a construction worker for the holidays to survive. The state of my mind was very depressing which almost led me to give up. On December 31st, 2012, it all came to an abrupt halt. I owed my roommate rent, and couldn't afford to pay. Unfortunately, I had to leave my place of residence forced to live on the streets. There it was New Year's Eve in the Big Apple, and I was homeless with no food, bed, or water. It felt like all my dreams were broken, and I have nothing left to live for. As I sat on the corner of 47th street in Manhattan, my mind began to brainstorm. My heart began to have a whirlwind of emotions twirling inside of it. Suddenly,

I came to an ultimatum which was to either continuing chasing my dreams or give up on everything. I chose my dreams! I got up off the curb, and headed towards the nearest homeless shelter I could find. On New Year's Eve, while everyone else was partying the night away I was being processed through intake at the largest emergency shelter in Manhattan. Once I was assigned a bed, I went straight to it.

I had to share a room with a complete stranger who I never met before. This man I will never forget because he truly inspired me. We stayed up all night talking about life. He told me his story of how he was a drug addict, on child support, and even let me know he was fighting with NY State for his disability checks.

He let me know that he was shot multiple times in his life, and had no remaining siblings who were alive. His ex wife, and children had moved to California over 10 years ago. After he was finished, I let him know my story as well. He wouldn't let me finish after 10 minutes because he was amazed at how a 19 year old had so much ambition. One important statement he told me was to "never quit, the only way you can lose as a dream chaser is if you quit."

In the morning, I woke up and he was gone. It was time for me to be placed in a shelter in the New York City area. All morning all I thought about was the conversation I had with the random stranger. The one night literally gave me a fresh start. Mentally, emotionally, and spiritually I felt revitalized. It was more than a coincidence for the moments that took place that evening.

I started January 1st, 2013 with no money but a heart full of ambition. Once I was given my assigned shelter, I left Manhattan to head to the Bronx. As I rode the subway to my destination, I started writing down the goals for 2013. I wrote down so many goals that it took 3 full pages. Next, I sorted my goals into long term and short term goals.

This allowed me to prioritize my objectives. Finally, I gave each goal I had a deadline. I learned a long time ago that goals without deadlines are like thoughts that never manifest into reality. The train arrived at my stop, and it was time to get off. I stepped off feeling more confident than I ever had felt before.

Emotions are the root of your soul. The way you feel affects how you think and act. In order to get to where you want to be at in life, you must keep control of your emotions. This means not letting any negativity overshadow your thoughts. Allowing yourself to feel negativity is like drinking poison from a cobra. You're killing yourself slowly, but surely. When you allow positive influences to affect your emotions then the opposite occurs.

Ambition is the fuel to your motivation. You have to make the best out of your situation no matter what. The driving force behind your life is going to be the energy you put into your destiny. Half hearted souls won't get much done as they procrastinate and make excuses frequently. Ambition is an intangible asset that will be a priceless source of energy as you move forward in your path.

It is very hard to stay motivated in a difficult environment. Motivation is connected to inspiration. If you desire to be more motivated about your future then you have to surround yourself around the right people along with the right environments. This will provide positive reinforcements in your life to sustain consistent motivation in your life.

Principles of Emotions, Ambition, and Motivation

1. **Emotional Success-** Every time you succeed in anything, your emotional response is what powers your momentum to be consistent. Emotional stability is one of the most important aspects of being successful. Winning and losing is not something you can always control. What you can control is your emotions. Focus on being successful at your emotional stability. This will translate over into your life tremendously.

2. **Ambition From Within- Harness** your power from within to fulfill your destiny. The purest form of excellence stems from the tree of prosperity. Enter your inner kingdom to become the Monarch that you are. The spirit of Ambition is attracted to hard workers. Laying the foundation to the castle is how you build an empire.

3. **Lion Motivation-** The motivation of a lion is one of fierce energy. A

penetrating force that breaks through every barrier in its way. The king of the jungle sits on its throne as a pure beast of nature. Your motivation can be of the same caliber. Unleash the inner beast within you. A mountain of issues can harass your life, but what allows you to overcome any adversity is motivation. Procrastination kills dedication! Look at the treasure map to find your way to the promise land. Knowledge evolves as technology grows. Accomplish your goals, and success will come to you.

Emotions are a cornerstone of the human psyche. What you feel affects your very existence. The beginning of your success will happen when you are ambitiously chasing your destiny with a fearless motivation. For thousands of years our culture has been built on the blood, sweat, and tears of our ancestors.

Open your mind to the possibilities that await you. Learn from history to enhance your future. Ambition brings out the fire that resides in your belly. Everyday that you are alive is another chance to make your dreams come true. You can't allow the competition to win! The winner of the war is the one who patiently preserves during each battle.

Your heart is the best weapon to use in the midst of tension. Grow your imagination beyond the average man. No one can stop you from being happy unless you allow them to. Motivation gives life to dreams. Bright minds can comprehend the challenge of being successful. Getting to the top is hard, but staying at the top is harder.

Find peace within your soul to balance your spiritual energy. The harmony of life relies on those amongst us who lead us to victory. Be the leader that you were born to be. Become inspired by the daily miracles that you see daily such as the sunrise, the smile on your mother's face, the crying of your child, and the breathe of fresh air that encompasses your very soul every morning you wake up. Believe and you will achieve.

Chapter 6
Intelligence Creates Wealth

The biggest achievement I have is my destiny. I believe everyday that I'm living my destiny because the source of my happiness comes from helping others. Regardless of what happens in my life I will always be happy. At 20, I moved from New York City to Atlanta. At this time, I really wanted to become successful due to the fact of me having a 3 year old son.

Everything in my life was about work. I was building 2 businesses with partners who I thought I could trust. In one summer so much transpired that it caught me off guard. I started the summer with a pocket full of cash, and two business partnerships that would eventually lead to my downfall. I realized that if I didn't free myself from the 100 hour work weeks my body would give out.

Throughout the summer of 2013 my income solely relied on entrepreneurship. I would stay awake for 3 nights straight working on an agenda that I couldn't escape. I was bouncing around the city of Atlanta making business moves trying to accomplish my goals. Everyday was a gut wrenching grind opportunities to get rich.

It was very difficult because I gave so much energy to my business that it affected my personal life. I had to give up my pleasures in order to survive. Regardless of my struggle I maintained a high confidence. I realized early on that it was going to take a long time to build an empire. No dynasty can be established overnight.

In September 2013, I decided to go back to my hometown Atlantic City for a break from the grind of Atlanta. I used the life experiences I learned while living down south to my advantage by creating a network of business contacts that I could utilize for income opportunities. The best part of networking is collaborating with like minds.

As an entrepreneur traveling was in my blood. Both of my parents are well traveled, and it had a strong effect on me growing up. I loved adventuring to new places. It was always an escape for me throughout my years of adolescence. The best part of traveling was networking. Throughout the years of my travels, I have met many amazing people which have led me to build many relationships throughout the world. The most important lesson I learned from building successful relationships is wealth distribution.

Building a network of contacts to create distribution channels of money is an extraordinary asset. Starting an investment portfolio will grow your business. In the beginning, every business suffers losses. The leaders who take control of bad situations are the ones who come out victorious. You have to plant the right seeds, and cultivate your money tree.

The corporate system of our society is built from capitalism. Everyone is either a producer, or a consumer. Taking control of your finances is the best move you can make. Invest your earnings into your business plan. Every entrepreneur needs a professionally and well documented business plan. Step into the realm of executive decision making. Be the boss you were born to be. My experiences have given me an abundance of knowledge which I grow daily. The ultimatum most of us are left with comes down to what we want versus what we need.

Sacrificing our desires for the betterment of our future is a daily goal that we must all accomplish. The hardship that comes with striving for greatness is merely a test. Stepping up to the plate when it is your time is the true testimony to success. You can be the water boy, or you can be a home run hitter.

People are emotional creatures. We all have primitive instincts that are influencing the way we live. Reacting to negative emotions will destroy your dreams. Finding the balance between your emotions, and thoughts is very important in order to sustain a high level of concentration. The biggest proposition you can accept is to develop your overall mental capacity. The amount of time you invest into yourself will vastly depend on the desire you have to attain greatness

Everyday is a new day, and you must fly your plan according to the weather you're traveling in. Putting your necessities first is an excellent way to improve your quality of life. Intelligence creates wealth by allowing us to learn how to make money work for us instead of us working for it. In a short amount of time, you can create what is needed to build a fortune. No one in this world can solely survive from money alone.

This is why it is important to gain assets with your money that show value over time. Income producing assets push our wealth forward regardless of how many hours we are working for a particular goal. In the beginning we look forward to the essential lives of our past generations for guidance for knowledge.

We accumulate this knowledge in our subconscious mind as it builds over time. By applying the right information to our lives we can expect to succeed by default. The biggest winners in life are using a blueprint that is now easily accessible through the internet, books, mentors, and more. You must seek knowledge, and apply what you learn to your life.

The world is a very mysterious place full of opportunity. You have to make the right decisions to get to the next level. In a very brief way, your life will flash before your eyes. The next thing you know you will be old with gray hairs saying where the time went. The time we get in our life is the most important asset we have because we don't get it back. You must make the right decisions at the right time to find the success you're looking for. Many people search far and wide but come up short on their goals because they don't make the cut when it comes to being a dream chaser.

A true sign of prosperity is being able to recognize opportunities when they present themselves. Seek guidance in your intelligence by consistently exercising your mind to become greater. Your mind is your greatest weapon. Learn how to use it to your advantage.

The biggest difference between those who succeed versus those who fail is the ones that use their brain correctly. Your intelligence is a vital part of everything you engage into. Keep your eyes open, and stay mentally alert on your journey of success.

Principles of Intelligence Creates Wealth

1. **Divine Intelligence** - We have the power to access another level of consciousness through our mental awareness. In order to tap into this realm you must conquer your subconscious mind by putting in place positive reinforcements to you help propel you forward in your journey. Divine intelligence is being in a peak state of mind.
2. **Thinking Everything Through** - One of the most calculated important aspects of using your mind is thinking things through. You must be strategic in every move you make to be successful in life. The bottom line is when you miss the mark due to not thinking things through it always winds up costing you more in the end.
3. **Work Smart** - In this world every move you make is about working smart. For decades there have been geniuses that reach the epitome of success because that focused their efforts while making smart choices.

Intelligence is a very important for all of us. Being smart about your life will be the reason you look back, and be proud of what you have accomplished. Your IQ level is not as important as you decision making abilities. Be intelligent about your decisions. Success Over Everything happens faster when you implement intelligence into your situation.

Don't let the negativity of this world make you an emotional wreck. Anger clouds good judgment. You must learn how to turn your anger into motivation by using your intelligence to do so. A helping hand is not far away. Get a mentor, or a person who can help you increase your intelligence so that you can master the craft of your choice. We all have the potential to become successful. What are you doing to make your success a reality?

Chapter 7
Being Wealthy

Becoming wealthy starts with you as a person. Your value can't be measured by monetary gain. If you add up all of your talents and skills you will come to find out that you're wealthy beyond measure. For a long time, I dealt with poverty at such a level it affected the way I saw the world. I didn't think I was worth anything let alone wealthy. I use to think God created me by mistake, and I am only here to be used by others. This was a very destructive mind set that could have led to my demise.

I woke up to the fact that many people who want to be successful don't have the right belief system in place to truly maximize all of their talents. You have to believe in yourself to get to the next level. Being wealthy is a lifestyle that you have to buy into one hundred percent.

In your pursuit of happiness, the wealth you acquire will come in many shapes and forms. To truly be wealthy, you must define what success will be for you. Our passion leads us towards the rivers of prosperity. Make a decision about your future, and stick to the plan.
I spent over a decade in perfecting my craft, and harnessing my talents.

I recognized at a very young age that becoming a business mogul was very important for me. Seeing my mother struggle pushed me to want more out of life than the average human being. I sacrificed whatever I had to in order to reach the goals I set for myself. A number of people have always compared me to the next Russell Simmons, Jay Z, or even Sean Combs. This comparison gave me more confidence because it allowed me to have a path to follow.

I knew in order to be wealthy; I had to study wealthy people. I had spent numerous hours upon hours reading books, blogs, magazines, and watching videos to train myself to become a mogul. I found mentors who gave me the right guidance I needed in order to progress further in my path. All of the time I invested in being a student of the game is paying off now. We often get the thought that we can succeed alone. While this sometimes may be true, it is more often you find wealthy people who have a team of people working for them. Wealthy people also surround themselves with like minded individuals.

Being wealthy is a life path you must choose to follow. A lot of us are at the fork in the road. We haven't decided on what path we want to take when it comes to being wealthy or poor. Wealth comes in three forms which are possessions, relationships, and knowledge. When you have all three forms of wealth working in your favor it allows you to be in a position to win big.

Principles of Being Wealthy

1. **Rich Mind** - A rich mind is an invaluable asset that you can easily acquire. You can turn your mind into a ocean of rich ideas. The best way to cultivate your mind is by applying the knowledge you have. Make the most out the information available to you. This will create a chain reaction that improves your mind's value over time.

2. **Rich Heart** - A rich heart is free from all negativity, malice, greed, or hatred. A heart in this form is truly a blessing. You can have a rich heart simply by giving unto others, being kind, and spreading love wherever you go.

3. **Rich Spirit** - A rich spirit has a vibrant energy about it that attracts others in abundance. Keep your faith strong, and allow God to bless you will make your spirit rich by default. The key is belief.

Exercise #1

Circle all of your attributes/traits

Critical Thinker	Fast Learner
Natural Leader	Strong Orator
Easy Going	Keen Intellect
Good Listener	Strong Instincts
Good Observer	Excellent Writer
Multi Talented	Extreme Athlete
Spiritually Aware	Positive Mindset
Impressive Style	Attractive Personality
Creative Genius	Great Attitude
Great Judgment	Strong Morals

Exercise #2
Answer the below questions

What will I do to be wealthy?

_____

_____

_____

_____

Why is being wealthy important to me?

_____

_____

_____

_____

_____

How will I become financially wealthy?

_____

_____

_____

_____

_____

Who are my biggest influences to be wealthy?

_____

_____

_____

_____

_____

Where am I going for my dream vacations, and why?

_____

_____

_____

_____

_____

What will I accomplish by being wealthy?

_____

_____

_____

_____

_____

Exercise #3

Complete The World Puzzle

```
t  d  n  t  c  z  m  r  i  c  h  n  w  y  g
a  l  h  b  q  b  g  g  d  n  y  b  z  m  s
l  m  k  u  s  k  i  l  l  s  x  u  e  l  u
e  a  v  s  l  l  z  w  e  a  l  t  h  y  q
n  n  y  i  f  r  s  f  z  a  l  n  g  t  w
t  s  t  n  y  a  k  o  h  c  g  g  j  e  i
v  i  d  e  i  x  m  a  r  r  i  a  g  e  c
h  o  f  s  o  w  n  i  t  y  c  o  o  n  h
c  n  m  s  n  d  y  i  l  h  e  e  l  u  a
e  a  s  s  e  t  s  n  m  y  w  s  p  m  r
m  o  g  u  l  h  x  b  s  w  y  r  y  l  i
l  f  s  l  p  i  l  s  q  g  b  g  r  o  t
d  n  m  b  i  l  l  i  o  n  a  i  r  e  y
f  t  d  a  m  i  l  l  i  o  n  a  i  r  e
t  c  o  n  f  i  d  e  n  c  e  l  i  e  r
```

charity
billionaire
wealthy
family
mansion
talent
mogul
tycoon
confidence
rich
business
millionaire
assets
skills
marriage

67

Chapter 8:
The Blueprint

In this final chapter, we will implement everything that was discussed in the book to create your blueprint of success. This is very important to have in place because it will be the plan that guides you regardless of what you are going through. Utilize this blueprint to be effective in your future to implement Success Over Everything.

<u>Vision Board</u>

Draw Your Innermost Desires of what success is for you.

Success Questions
Answer Each Question

What will I do to be successful?

_____

_____

_____

_____

_____

Why am I going to be successful?

_____

_____

_____

_____

_____

How will I become successful in my life?

_____

_____

_____

_____

_____

Who will I become successful with, and why?

_____

_____

_____

_____

_____

The Success Grid

Fill in the grid with your own success words in the white spaces until completely full.
The objective is to connect your words horizontally, vertically, and diagonally.
Then write all the words you spelled out below the grid.
Ex. You spell Rich horizontally on the first column, and the use the R to spell Real vertically.

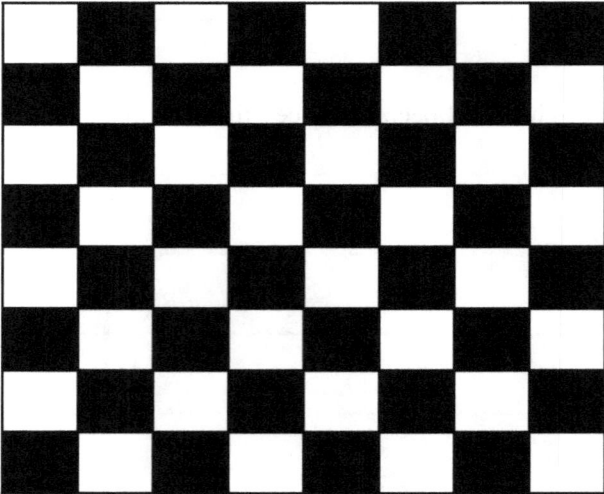

Words
_____

_____

Success Priorities

List your success priorities in numerical order.

1.

2.

3.

4.

5.

6.

7.

8.

9.

10.

<u>Goals</u>

List your goals, and give a deadline to each goal listed.

Short Term Goals	Deadline
Long Term Goals	**Deadline**

The Perfect Story

*Write a short story on of how you would want
your life story to be told by others*

_____

_____

_____

_____

_____

_____

_____

_____

_____

_____

_____

_____

Bonus Section
Wealth Trends

The following are wealth trends in the world we live in described in detail:

1. Real Estate - Real Estate Investing has created more millionaires than any other industry in the world.

2. Technology - Technology is a very common wealth trend because it allows you to explore a world of advancement and innovation. Technology ranges from building software applications, to creating the best new hardware, or even to create a worldwide new invention.

3. Entertainment- We find a lot more people pursuing entertainment for the quest to become a world renowned figure. Entertainment can be a very lucrative endeavor if done correctly.

4. Fashion- The fashion world is a great wealth trend which has existed for centuries. Countless designers and models have reached an epitome of success because of having trendy looks

and ideas. You can reach new heights of success if create a strong fashionable brand that people love.

5. Stocks Market - The Stock Market is an amazing way to become an investor, and create a profitable passive cash flow for your portfolio. The stock market has created various forms of income for many far and wide. Be very careful, not to dive right into the stock market without doing your research. You must be financially stable to enter the stock market at any stage.

Disclosure
The wealth trends mentioned in the bonus section are completely the opinion of the author. In by no way shape or form is there an expression, or guarantee of any monetary gain by following the the advice given in the wealth trends bonus section. Seek a lawyer for legal advice, and seek a certified public account for tax advice.

Author Biography

Joshua Armah is a renowned entrepreneur, consultant, motivational speaker, author, and capitalist. Born in the world famous Atlantic City, NJ he was raised by a single mother who did her best to give him a bright future. Despite her efforts, Joshua Armah's curiosity got the best of him which led him to journey into the devil's playground.

As a teenager, Joshua Armah went through many trials and tribulations which almost cost him his life. At 14 years old, he ran away from home to live a life in the streets. He has experienced the world of thugs and gangsters to the extreme. He was attracted to a flashy lifestyle, and the fast paced action in the ghetto.

As a young hustler he did what he had to do in order to survive in the concrete jungle. He faced many vices from gangs, drugs, violence, homelessness, domestic abuse, peer pressure, and poverty. These experiences put a chip on his shoulder at a very early age.

At the age of 16, Joshua was faced with a life changing situation. His girlfriend at the time had become pregnant with a boy. This situation woke Joshua up from a mental slumber.

The sequence of events to follow who alter his life forever. He decided to walk away from High School to pursue his GED through NJ Youth Corps. After completing the program, he enrolled in college to study Business Administration. He went on to change his life and give up the negative habits of his past for a brighter future. For two years, he worked 3 sales oriented jobs and attended college while taking care of his new family. During this time, a pivotal flame erupted in his heart which gave him the inspiration to pursue a career as an entrepreneur.

Unfortunately, another obstacle would present itself in his path to greatness. After finally becoming 18 years old, an unforeseen occurrence happened to Joshua. His wife committed infidelity, and left him for another man. Due to his survival instincts Joshua decided to continue on his path. At this time, Joshua had no one to turn to so he became homeless once again. Fighting everyday to eat, shower, sleep, and work.

He lost his employment, and was unable to complete college due to his financial hardships. This took a big toll on his motivation. Out of the blue, a miracle happened. A close friend called Joshua to check on him to see how he was doing. After Joshua explained his situation, his friend told him to move in immediately. This experience was very important because it allowed Joshua to start from scratch. Joshua began employment hunting, and by the grace of God found an opportunity with a fortune 500 company.

This opportunity allowed Joshua to get back on his feet to continue his dreams of entrepreneurship. After spending less than a year in corporate America, Joshua Armah left to New York City to fulfill his dream of entrepreneurship. He spent a lot of time consulting, and working with major brands. He eventually was led into the entertainment industry where he sought to make his mark as a fierce competitor.

By working with the right mentors, Joshua found himself as a rising Entrepreneur in the Big Apple. Many people took notice to his skill set and abilities. Left and right, new opportunities were being sent his way

. Joshua took advantage of everything that New York City had to offer. He went on to become a Executive Vice President for a Talent Agency, and helped run a management firm. During the course of his tenure he signed celebrity acts to the agency while working the the firm to provide solutions to small businesses.

To date, Joshua Armah has owned and operated 3 companies in a c level executive position. He has worked with Inc 5000 and Fortune 500 companies. He has consulted for over 100 brands. He has also generated over 1.5 million in revenue for various clients combined.

He promotes the motto "Success Over Everything" in which he inspires many through motivational speaking. His professional experience extends from real estate, business consultation entertainment, brand management, network marketing, communications, sales, customer acquisition, and much more. Joshua currently resides in Atlanta, GA where he is expanding into new ventures. His mission is to change the world through actions one step at a time. By being proactive, Joshua is set to fulfill his destiny and be a leader for the next generation.

www.ingramcontent.com/pod-product-compliance
Lightning Source LLC
Chambersburg PA
CBHW071627040426
42452CB00009B/1526